# BABY'S WORLD

## ANGELA WILKES

DK

**DORLING KINDERSLEY**

London • New York • Stuttgart

DK

A Dorling Kindersley Book

**Design** Mathewson Bull
**Photography** Stephen Shott
**Managing Art Editor** Roger Priddy

First published in Great Britain in 1990
by Dorling Kindersley Limited,
9 Henrietta Street, London WC2E 8PS
Reprinted 1990, 1991, 1993

A CIP catalogue record for this book is available
from the British Library.

ISBN 0-86318-423-5

Reproduced by Bright Arts, Hong Kong
Printed and bound in Italy by Graphicom

Additional photography by Stephen Oliver
(pages 34 - 35) and Dave King (pages 36 - 37)

Dorling Kindersley would like to thank:
Hamish Anderson, Roxanne Bance,
Christian Harman, Troy Hunter, Holly Jackman,
Rebecca Langton, Emily Morrison, Sam Priddy,
Kerra Stevens and Aaron Wong for
appearing in the photographs in this book;
Boots the Chemist Limited and
Jacadi Limited for loaning props.

# Contents

# Me

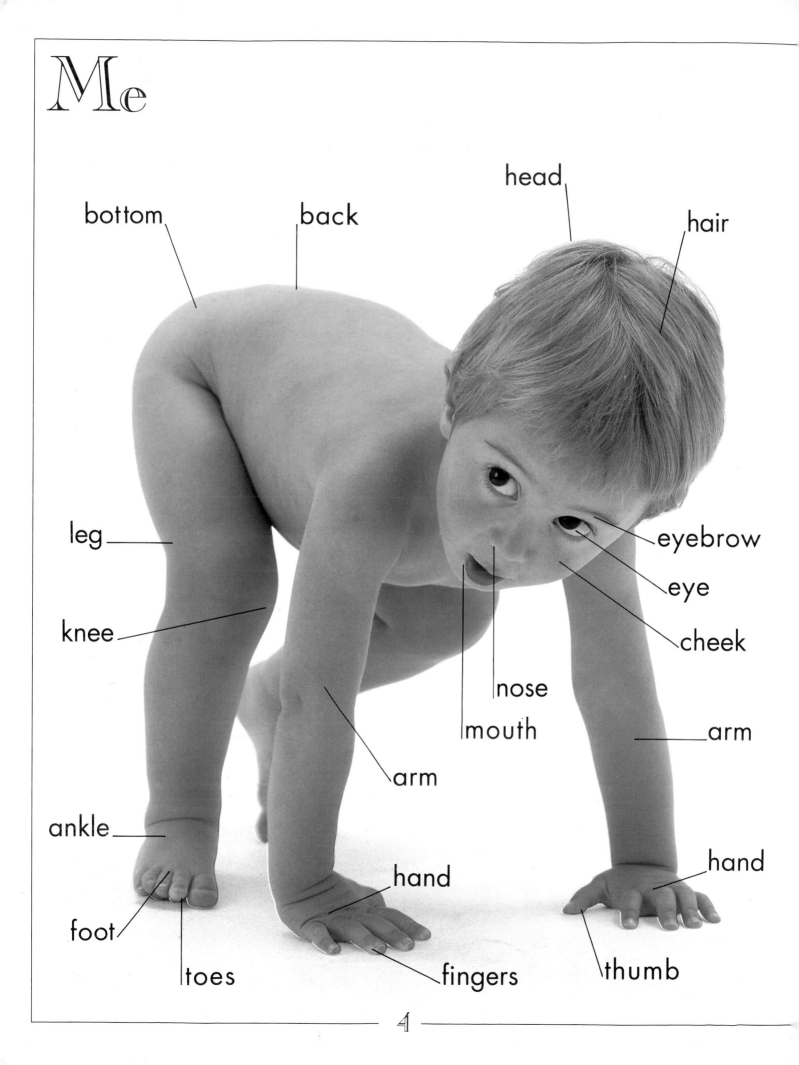

bottom

back

head

hair

leg

knee

eyebrow

eye

cheek

nose

mouth

arm

arm

ankle

hand

hand

foot

toes

fingers

thumb

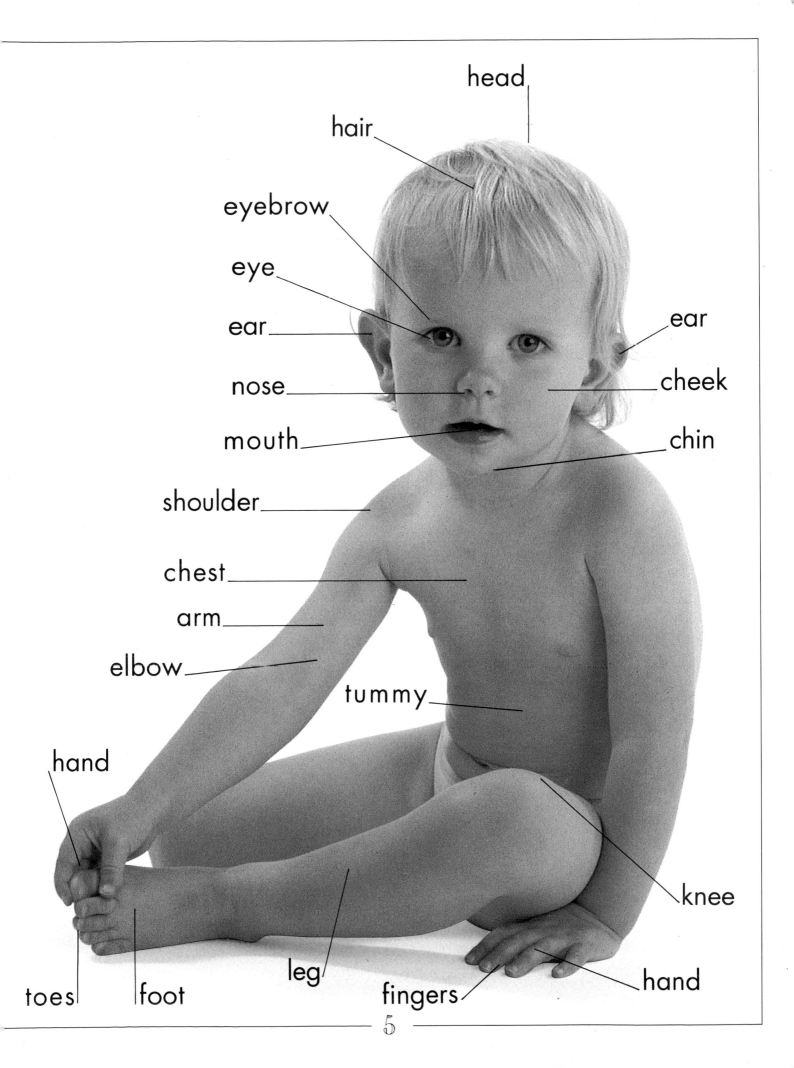

head

hair

eyebrow

eye

ear

nose

mouth

shoulder

chest

arm

elbow

tummy

hand

ear

cheek

chin

knee

toes

foot

leg

fingers

hand

5

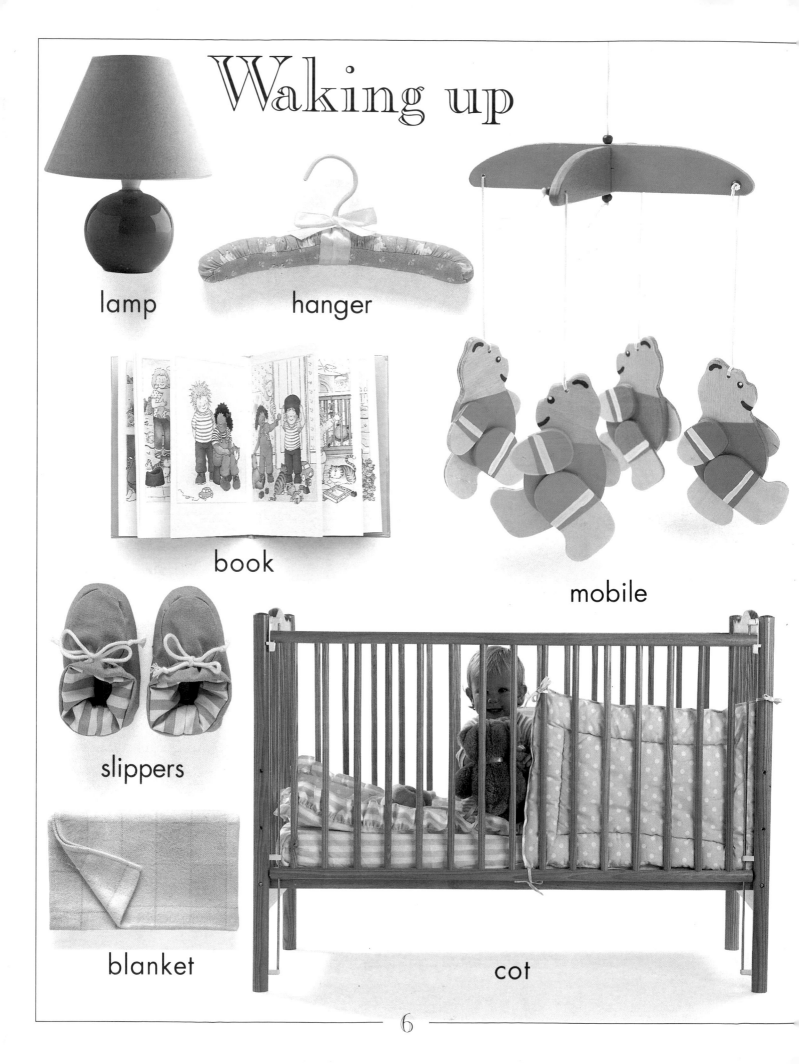

# Waking up

lamp

hanger

book

mobile

slippers

blanket

cot

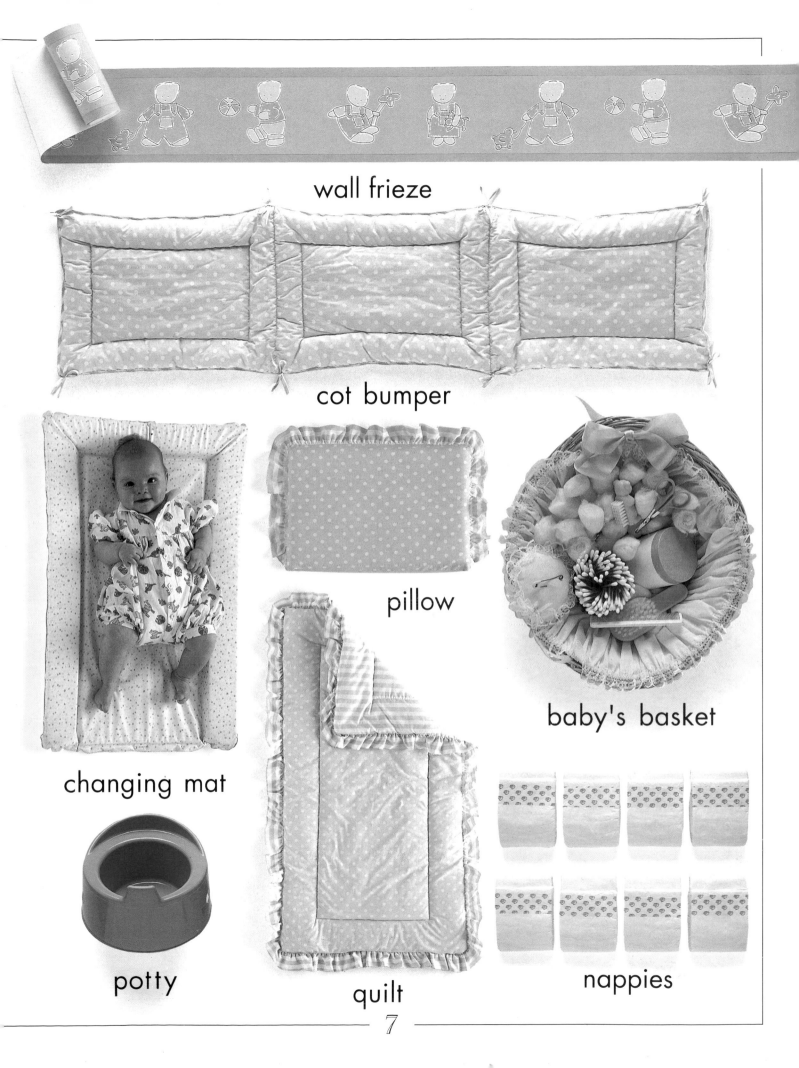

wall frieze

cot bumper

pillow

baby's basket

changing mat

potty

quilt

nappies

7

# My clothes

sunhats

rompers

tee shirt

shirt

shorts

dungarees

babystretch

vest

pants

socks

baby shoes

baby boots

shoes

8

woolly hat

scarf

dress

jacket

trousers

mittens

jumper

socks

playshoes

slippers

shoes

boots

9

# Getting dressed

1. When Sam wakes up, he is wearing his sleepsuit.

2. Now he has nothing on.

6. Now Sam is in his dungarees.

7. He pulls on his socks.

8. Then he puts on his shoes.

3. His nappy is put on.

4. Then his vest.

5. And then his shirt.

9. He has a quick chat with his teddy bears.

10. Then up he gets, ready for breakfast.

# Eating and drinking

Here are all the different things you use at mealtimes.
How many forks? Which colours can you see?
How many bibs can
you count?

bottles

bibs

bowls

spoons

forks

beakers

cups

bibs

bowls

# Mealtime

All the babies are in their highchairs.

Peter is playing with his food.

Christian is drinking from his cup.

They sit in their highchairs
every mealtime.

Sarah is eating
her biscuit.

Tom is drinking
from his bottle.

# My toys

doll

teddy bears

beakers

puzzle

activity centre

soft bricks

16

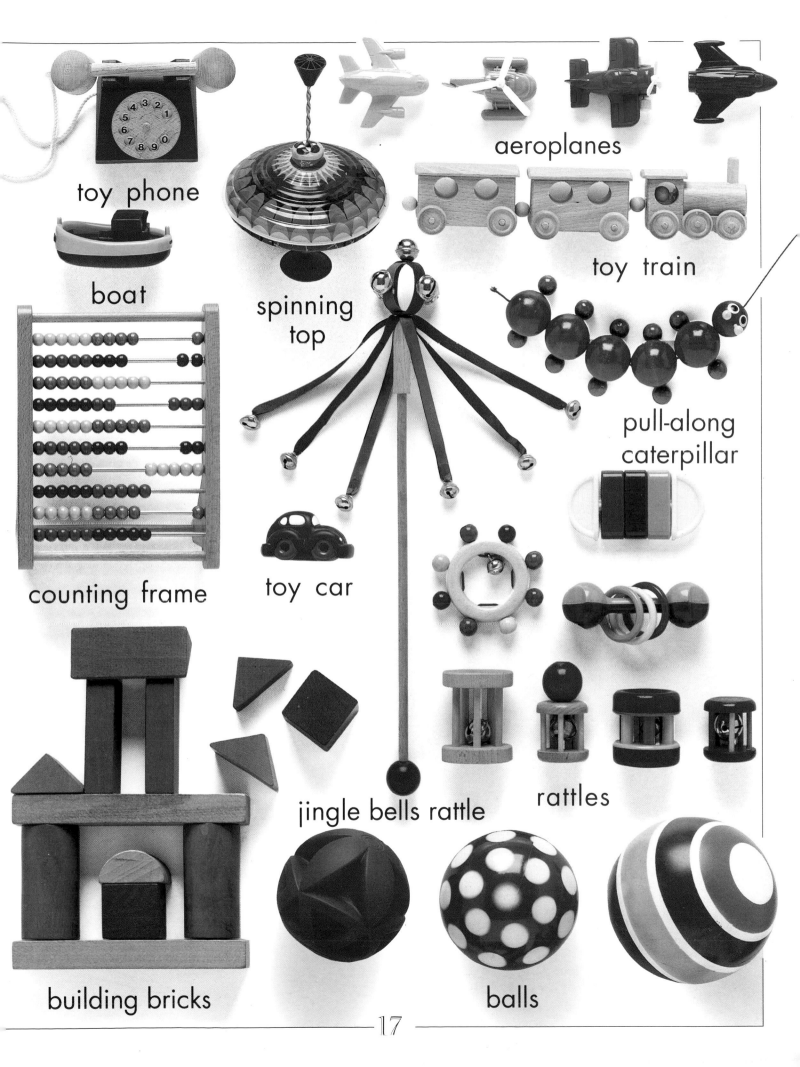

toy phone

aeroplanes

boat

toy train

spinning top

pull-along caterpillar

counting frame

toy car

jingle bells rattle

rattles

building bricks

balls

# Toys that go

pull-along caterpillar

push-along duck

18

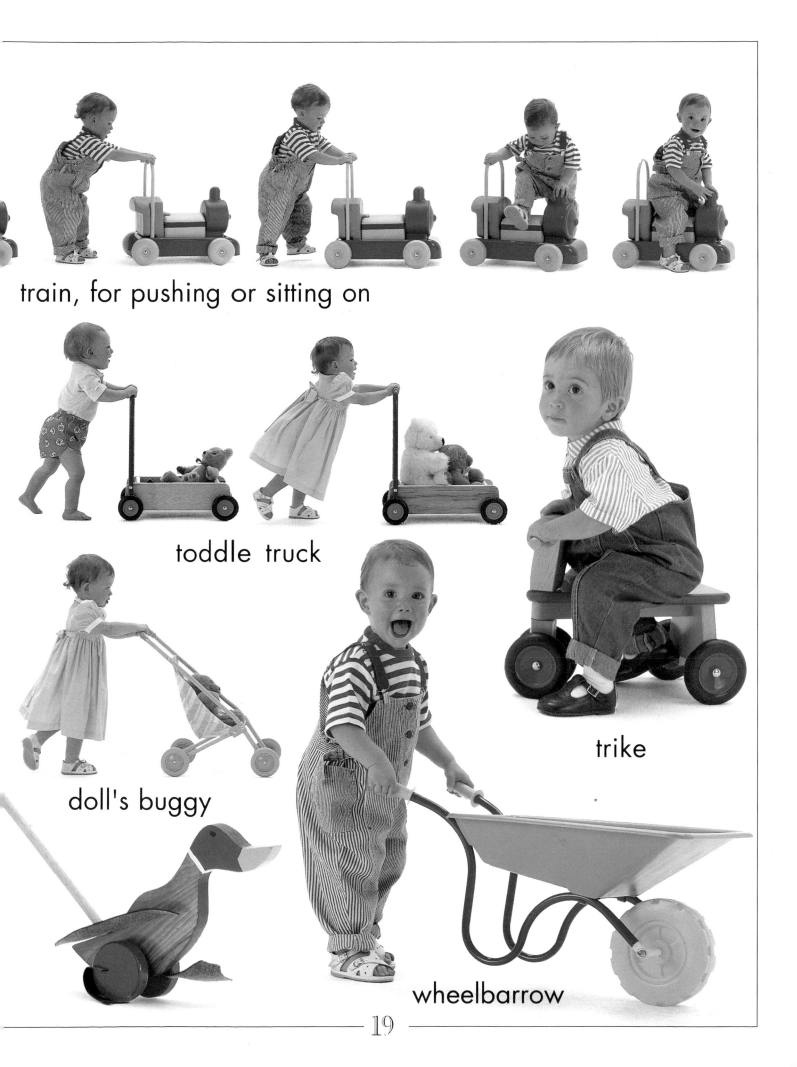

train, for pushing or sitting on

toddle truck

doll's buggy

trike

wheelbarrow

19

# Colours

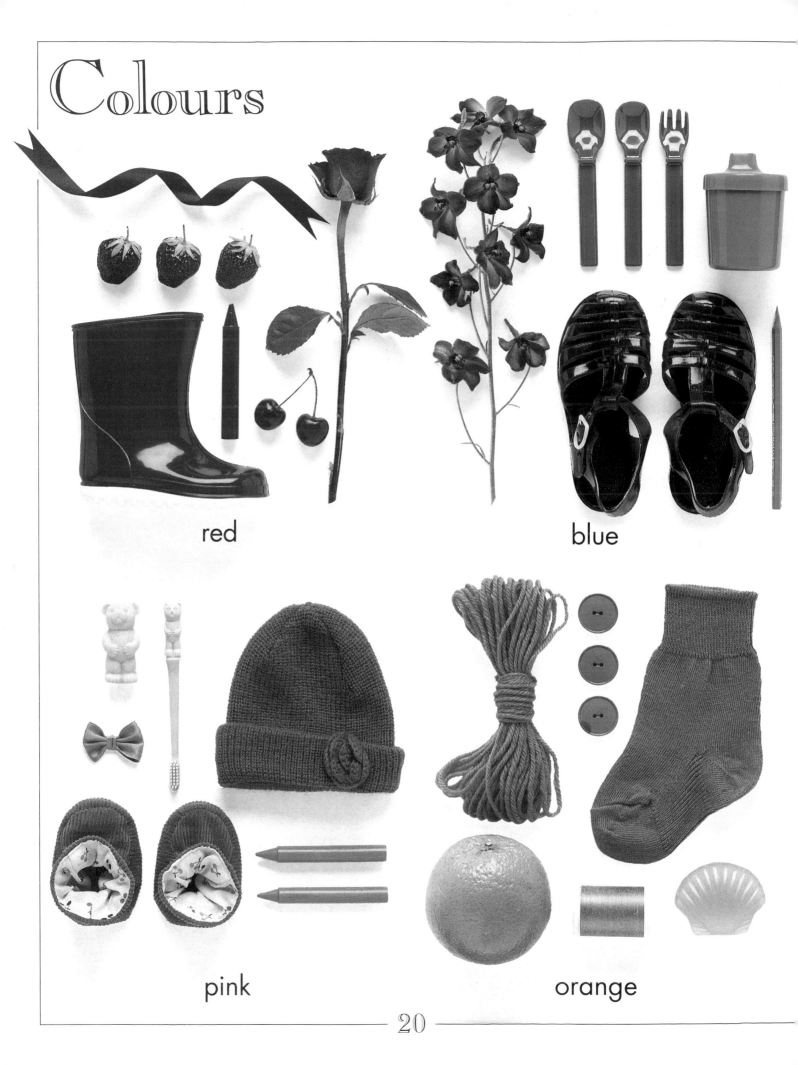

red

blue

pink

orange

yellow

green

purple

brown

# Pets

kittens

goldfish

puppies

birds

rabbit

cat

# Moving about

kicking

sitting

lying down

crawling

sitting and playing    kneeling    crouching

getting up    walking    standing

# Out and about

Babies go out in buggies all the year round.
They go out in the sun, the rain and the snow.

Warm days

Sunny days

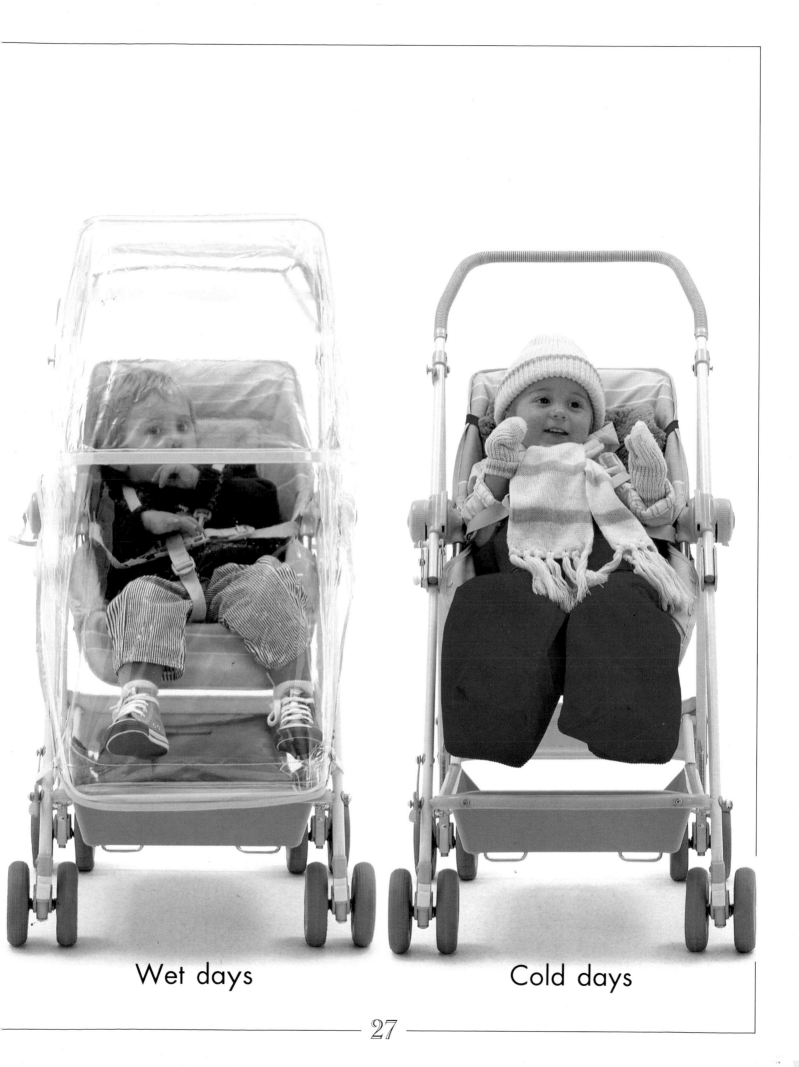

Wet days

Cold days

# Things to eat

cherries

peach

banana

strawberries

orange

grapes

apple juice

apple

blackcurrant drink

tomato

yogurt

animal biscuits

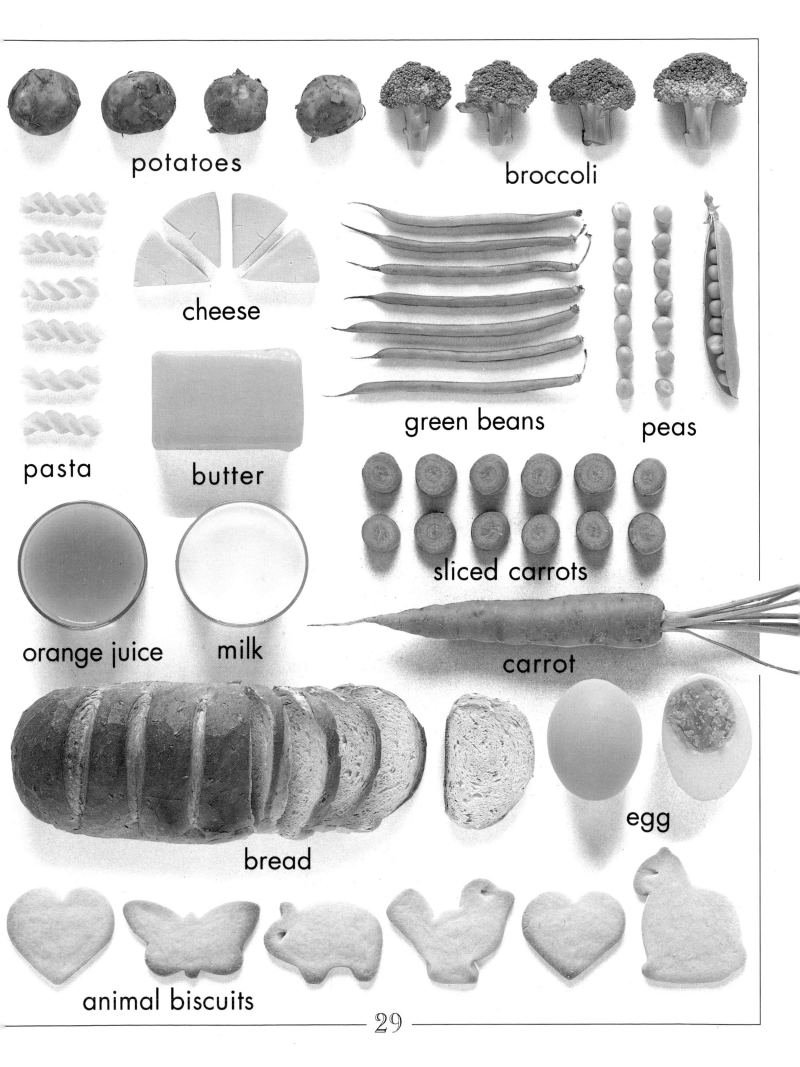

potatoes

broccoli

cheese

green beans

peas

pasta

butter

sliced carrots

orange juice

milk

carrot

bread

egg

animal biscuits

# In the garden

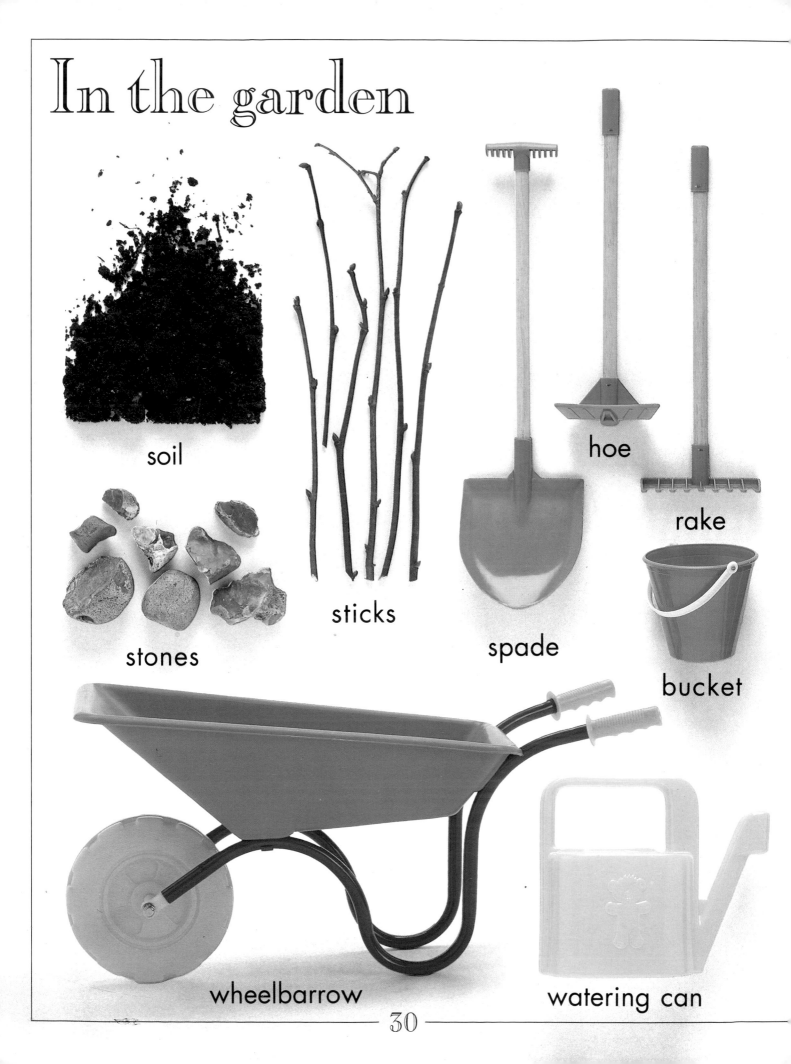

soil

sticks

hoe

rake

stones

spade

bucket

wheelbarrow

watering can

leaves

snail

flowers

plants

flowerpots

31

# Sand play

The babies are in the sandpit.
They are playing with
buckets and spades.

Sam

teddy bear
mould

ball

How many toys can you see?

parasol

Hamish

bucket

spade

Sarah

buckets

spade

Rebecca

beakers

33

# Bathtime

soap dish

safety pins

bubble bath

shampoo

soaps

towels

beakers

bath ducks

sponges

cotton wool

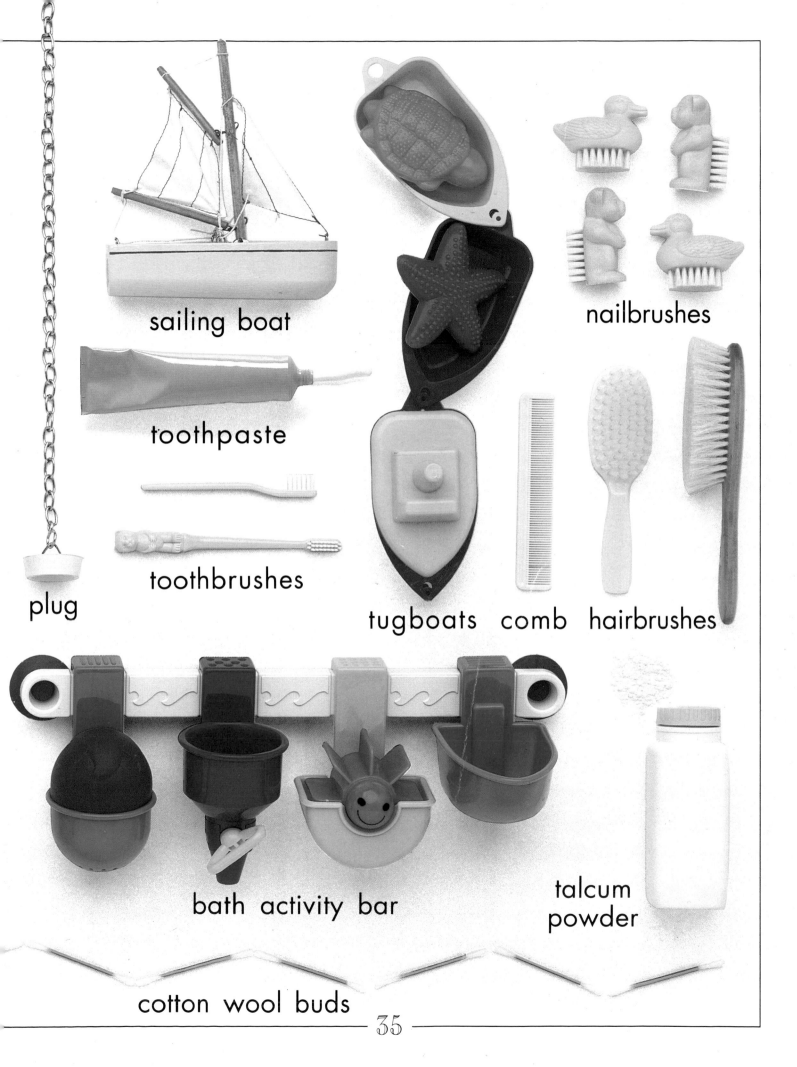

sailing boat

toothpaste

toothbrushes

plug

nailbrushes

tugboats    comb    hairbrushes

bath activity bar

talcum
powder

cotton wool buds

# In the bath

The bath is full of toys.
Which toys can you see?
How many ducks can you count?
Can you see the soap and the sponge?

# Going to bed

1. Holly is tired. It is bedtime.

2. She takes off her shoes.

3. She pulls off her socks.

7. Now Holly is in her sleepsuit.

8. She is sleepy and rubs her eyes.

9. Time for a quick drink.

4. Holly takes off
   her dress.

5. Off comes
   her vest.

6. And on comes a
   clean nappy.

10. Then Holly is put in her cot.
    Goodnight!

# Counting

**1** one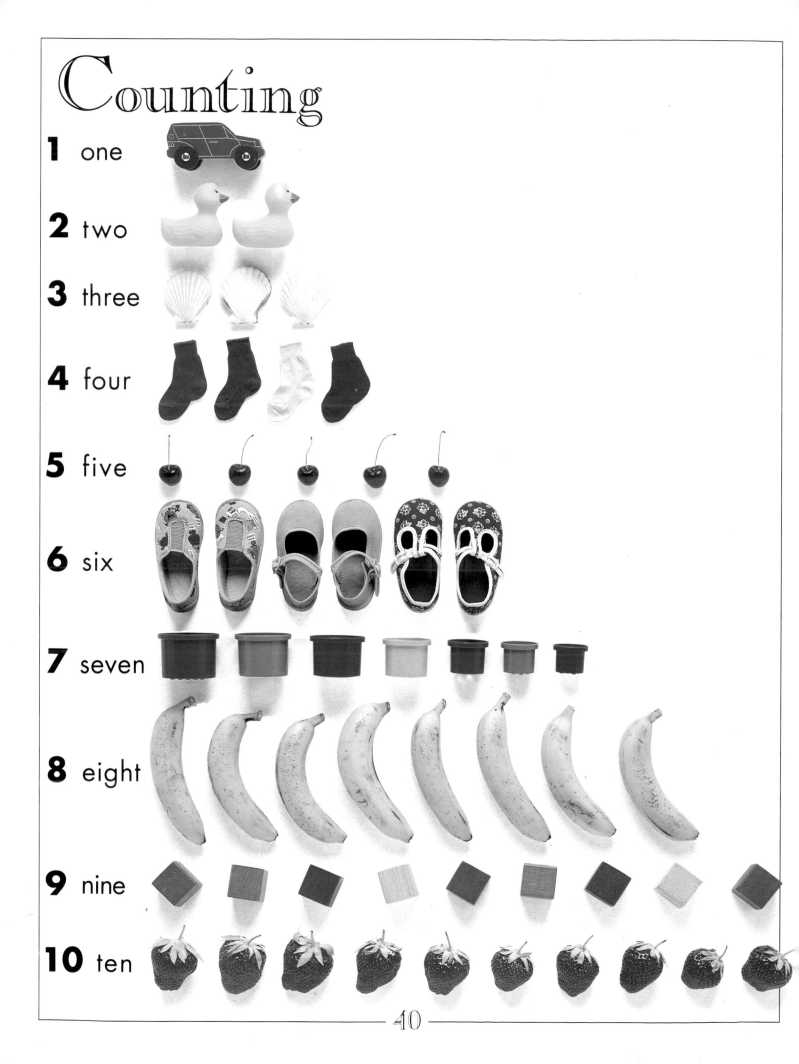

**2** two

**3** three

**4** four

**5** five

**6** six

**7** seven

**8** eight

**9** nine

**10** ten